JMC 02 0209 110

Class No. .... Acc. No. ....

Branch

Leabharlann na Mí
(Meath County Library)

9 2002

Loan period — two weeks.

A fine of 25p per week or part of week is charged on overdue books.

WITHDRAWN FROM STOCK

WITHDRAWN FROM STOCK

14. 09.

18.

0 6 MAY 2010

1 8 NOV 2010

2 3 MAR 2013

1 4 SEP 2013

1 8 MAR 2016

D0492671

A Day in the Life of a...

Train Driver

Harriet Hains

W

FRANKLIN WATTS

NEW YORK•LONDON•SYDNEY

J/385 /1705905

Terry is a train driver. He drives the Eurostar train from London, in England to Paris, in France. Terry starts his day at 7.30 a.m. when he arrives at Waterloo International Terminal.

Leabharlann
Contae na Mídhe

2

First Terry goes to the Control Room. He uses an electronic card to 'swipe on' duty for the day.

Then Terry collects a radio so he can talk to controllers in London and Paris.

3

Next Terry collects
his bag from the
locker room.
Then he looks
for any special
notices about the
trains or tracks
on that day.

Meanwhile, passengers are arriving at the station. Liam and Kate are going to Paris for the day with their mum and dad. "Look, the train leaves at 8.53 a.m.," says Liam.

On the platform, Terry makes sure
his train is ready for the journey.
He checks that the brake lights at the back
are working and that the computer in the
back cab is switched on.

"Everything is ready now," Terry says to himself, as he climbs into the driver's cab.

At 8.30 a.m. the passengers start to board the train. "May I see your tickets, please?" the Steward asks the passengers.
"Your seats are just to the left."

Inside the cab, Terry checks
the computers and brakes.
At 8.53 a.m. a green signal
tells Terry that it is time
to leave Waterloo.

"How long is the journey to Paris?" asks Liam.
"It takes only three hours," Kate tells him.
The children play games and spot places of
interest as the train goes by.

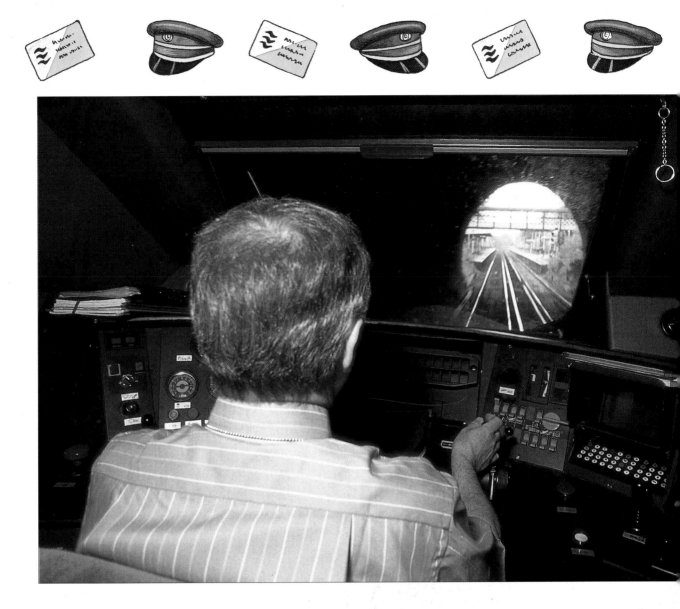

Terry drives the train through the English countryside to Ashford. There are small tunnels on the way. After Ashford, the train enters the Channel Tunnel and goes under the sea.

Once the train is out of the Channel Tunnel, it is in France. Terry talks to the French controllers on the radio. Then he tells the passengers how fast the train is going. Terry says the message first in French, then he repeats it in English.

At 12.53 p.m., the train arrives at the Gare du Nord station in Paris. "Hurray!" says Liam. "It's time for some more fun."

13

Terry and other Eurostar staff go to a restaurant to relax and have lunch.
"The food here is delicious, isn't it?"
Terry says.

Later Terry returns to the station to drive the 4.07 p.m. train back to London.
"There are no problems," says the French Platform Controller. So the train leaves on time.

Soon Terry is driving back through
the Channel Tunnel into England.
"Next stop is Ashford," he says to himself.

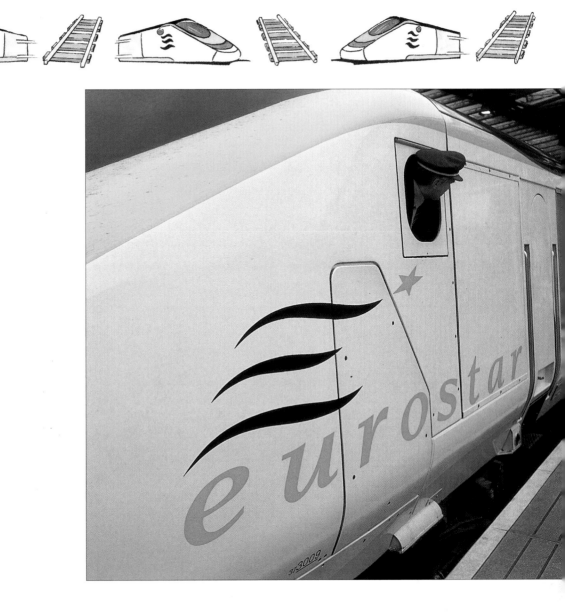

At Ashford station, Terry checks with the Platform Controller that they are ready to go.

It's 6.13 p.m. and Terry arrives back at Waterloo station in London. When everyone is off the train, Terry goes to 'book off' duty.

18

Terry puts his case back in his locker ready for the next day. "Now it's time to drive myself home," he says.

The Eurostar train journey

This map shows the journey of the Eurostar from **London** to **Paris**. The area marked in blue is the sea.

How long was the journey from London to Paris?
Did the train stop at any other stations on the way?

Make a map of your own favourite train journey.

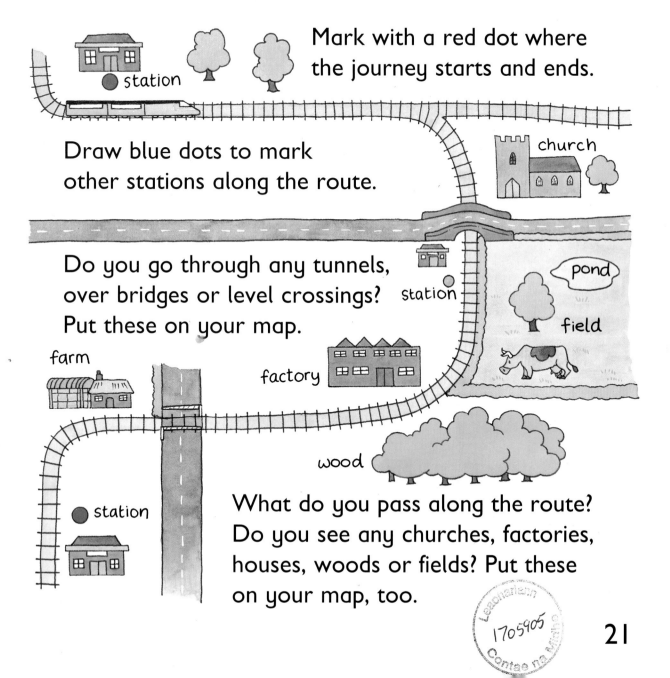

Mark with a red dot where the journey starts and ends.

Draw blue dots to mark other stations along the route.

Do you go through any tunnels, over bridges or level crossings? Put these on your map.

What do you pass along the route? Do you see any churches, factories, houses, woods or fields? Put these on your map, too.

1705905

21

Facts about Eurostar

1. The journey from London to Paris takes 3 hours. There is one hour's time difference between London and Paris. When it is 8.53 a.m. in London it is 9.53 a.m. in Paris.

2. The Eurostar can travel up to 300 kilometres per hour.

3. The train driver and the staff on the train speak both English and French. They announce information in both languages.

4. The drivers carry luminous vests and lamps so that they can be seen clearly in case they have to go onto the tracks.

Facts about train drivers

All train drivers are specially trained. They have to know how their train works and they have to be very fit and healthy. They have to take tests to make sure that they can drive safely during the day or night. They also have to keep on time. Nobody likes it when a train is late!

There are different types of train drivers.

Trainees: All train drivers start as trainees. They learn about controls and tracks and take many tests. Then they are allowed to drive a train with an experienced trainer. They learn to obey signals and drive at the correct speed. After some more tests, they can become a Train Driver.

Train Drivers: Drivers learn about different stations and signals on many routes. They drive trains carrying passengers or goods. These trains can be either diesel or electric. Some drivers drive through the night to deliver the mail.

International Drivers: These drivers learn to drive the Eurostar trains to France and Belgium that go through the Channel Tunnel. They have to learn to speak French so that they can pass messages on to Controllers and Signallers on the journey.

Index

© 1999 Franklin Watts

Franklin Watts
96 Leonard Street
London
EC2A 4RH

Franklin Watts Australia
14 Mars Road
Lane Cove
NSW 2066

ISBN: 0 7496 3312 3

Dewey Decimal Classification
Number: 385

10 9 8 7 6 5 4 3 2 1

A CIP catalogue record for
this book is available from the
British Library.

Printed in Malaysia

Editor: Samantha Armstrong
Designer: Louise Snowdon
Photographer: Chris Fairclough
Illustrations: Nick Ward

With thanks to: Debbie and Liam
Clark, James Eaton, Kate Harrison
and everyone at Eurostar UK.